# THE WINNING MINDSET FOR LIFE AND BUSINESS

## JOHN H.OLSEN

20Twenty
Literary Group

ISBN
978-1-962868-85-3 (Paperback)
978-1-962868-86-0 (eBook)
978-1-962868-84-6 (Hardcover)

Olsen

# Table of Contents

# OLSEN

## The winning mindset
## For life and business

To my dad and mom

Albert Olsen Jr. and Viola D. Olsen.

# Viking Code

Protect your family

Honor your elders

Teach your young

Be loyal to your friends

Voice your opinion

Stand your ground

Take charge when others show weakness

Play when you can

Work when you must

Always leave your mark

*My surname is my brand but I don't own it. It is borrowed from my ancestors.*

*I must return it unstained. My honor is not my own. It is on loan from my descendants.*

*I must give it back unbroken. Our blood is not our own.*

*It is a gift generations yet to be born. We should carry it with responsibility.*

-Vincent Enlund

# Introduction

What is success and do people define success for themselves. Success for each person and how they achieve that success is different for each person. Success can be a matter of a person's mindset that they have. State of mind is something a person has to work each and every day. Writing it down and telling it to yourself that you deserve to be wealthy on a daily basis and that you believe it. You have it wrote down, and you can observe it on a daily basis. Clarity starts with your own mind.

I have read lots of books and they try defining success for you. Thing is success means different things to different people. For me early on was trying to find and get a job because when I was growing up jobs were hard to come by. I grew up in a farming area of the state, and that was all I ever knew and was taught growing up in how to work on a farm. The meaning of success has evolved as I have gotten older after having struggled and lived paycheck to paycheck. That is when I decided to go into the military after I was married, but the struggles still continued during my military career.

I admired my dad and wanted to be with him and learn from him everything I could learn. I was his helper on several construction jobs and he was my mentor. That is why I was shocked when one day he told me that I wouldn't amount to anything and that my little brother would amount to more.

That is when I set out to prove to him I could be a success and a lot better than my little brother. Finding and surrounding yourself with people that will help and support you in all that you want to achieve and to be. The vision and dream is there and it is being built one block at a time. I am learning all that I can about what I want to do with my life. Success is achieved one step at a time through hard work and a successful vision.

Part of that successful vision was to invest in things that I understood like successful blue chip businesses that have been around for a very long time.

Communication is a key quality in any success that you want to achieve, because if you are not able to clearly communicate your vision to others then how are they to support you successfully. Communication and being about your vision lets those around you help you and keep you on track toward that goal you had set-up for yourself.

The military had their way to build your mindset and reinforce that mindset each and every day. They also used it to build team work amongst all the shipmates. They did this by making us exercise each day and when someone had done something wrong, because they wanted us to work as one unit. I do have those times when my mind slips back into an old mindset that can be destructive and non-motivating. A strong mindset has helped me move forward since 2008 and being on my own since my mom has passed away.

My brand is my surname. A surname I get from my family that I carry with honor. A brand that lives by its core values that I learned from family, and from my time in the U.S. Navy. I also learned a lot when I was a teen mowing lawns for different people and sometimes if I didn't want to mow the lawn for some reason. Once you start making excuses about you not wanting to do something, and now those excuses come easier and easier as time goes on. The great thing about the Navy is though they don't let you get away with those excuses and they would hold you accountable for your excuses and actions.

It has also helped me get my degree in Business Administration Accounting that I had started when I was in the US Navy a degree that had taken me over ten years to finally complete. It has kept me moving forward in life and in my college studies. I was forced to drop my last quarter of college but when I can I will go back to college and get my Associate of Science degree in Computer Drafting and Design. If you have a strong mind and if you stick to it and everything that is worthwhile you can achieve, but you have to be tough and strong.

Amongst those strengths is your character and like your mindset it can help you achieve great things. One thing that I have never forgotten and it has helped strengthen my character was the time I got in trouble with my Grandmother Hoyt. She caught me in a lie and she spanked me for lying to her which now I feel I deserved to get because I lied to her. The US Navy also used the same method to build the persons character along with their mindset and team work. Part of one's character how they handle failure and how they overcome failure and the setback. I often wonder if I didn't get my strength of character from my Norwegian ancestors. I have learned and I do understand more about my Norwegian ancestors.

Pulling together your mindset and strength of character to build a strong and a successful brand. It all started when I was mowing lawns, but I didn't fully understand what it all meant at the time. I didn't have the teacher or the mentor at the time to teach me at the time about a brand and how to build a brand. My dad never finished school and my mom only knew what she was taught in school. They had no way of teaching me what I needed to know about the business side of life, other than work for a paycheck which I have my entire life.

I started my own little cattle operation and now I was reasonable for their welfare and wellbeing. Now in a way they were holding me accountable for them, which made me more reasonable of a person. I had bigger dreams for the business, but working for the dairy wasn't going to get me toward my goal. I ended up selling the cows and shelving the dream of owning my own business. That is why I needed a partner that would have worked with me and not against me in a defeating way.

I have gone back to college to learn all I can to help build that foundation for a successful dream. I have already started laying the foundation toward a successful business, and that has also been

gaining the much needed business contacts that can help me along the way. They will also help strengthen my business and personal network. While surrounding myself with positive and high energy people that will keep energized and motivated to keep going. The strength of the network can help you find and get the good deals that are out there and sometimes you have to be able to act very fast before that deal slips away from you.

That is why a lot of deals are a matter of timing and being in the right place at the right time. That is why a strong and great network is so important to your business, but is not only about the network to get the good deals. You have to have the means to secure those good deals and that means being financially secure. What use is a great network if you don't have the financial means to get the deals that come your way? Then the network you have built is worthless.

That is part of building a good foundation to work from, and that is why the littlest of things thing's matter because that can also mean the difference between wither you get that loan for that property you are just trying to buy. That is also why your credit is so important to you, and a lot of people take that for granted. It is even more important post 2008. It is also that your winning mind set be in alignment with you as a whole with your inner most truth inside of you.

# Chapter 1

## Meaning of success

What is success and how do you define success. Success is one of those words joy and happiness. You can talk to different people what they think the meaning of success and each one of the will come up with a different meaning for success. For some people they could spell success as just living comfortable each and every day with what they have. For some people they could spell success by how much money they have. Most all parents' success is to them. It is to see their kids are better off than they were in their lives. Then they want their kids to be better off than their parents.

I have seen lots of books written on success and how to achieve that success. To me there is no magic formula for achieving success, even though some people will say they have the keys to get you there. Each one of us has a different way of achieve success for them, and it holds a different meaning for them. To every person there is a different meaning of success to them. My question to you is how do you spell success to you?

For me early on in my life success to me was finding a job and earning enough money to buy whatever I wanted. I thought about the then now and I wasn't thinking about the future. The meaning of success for me has evolved has I have gotten older and thought about what the meaning of my life could be. I had seen my parents' lives and how much they had to struggle just for the basics in life. After haven analyzed their life, I knew I wanted more then to just get by from paycheck to paycheck. Taking any and every job that came my way even though I wasn't happy with the job. I thought the military could help put me on that path for success, but little did I know I would be right back where I started from before I joined the military.

I made an ok living in the military, but still I wouldn't define it as successful. The reason why I say it wasn't successful, because I had to continue to struggle to just get by. Living from paycheck to paycheck isn't success. I would define success in my life as not having to struggle or worry if my basic needs are going to be met that month. I was still making more than I did if I had stayed working on the farm. Then again I always did like the country way of life that I had grown up on.

I admired my dad and wanted to be around him and learn all I could from him. I helped my dad build a fence; remodel a house with his brother, and a play house. I also built many other things with my dad. I learned how to set siphon tubes to irrigate a hay field from him. I learned many other things from my dad over the years. I used what I had learned from my dad when I went to work for Dave Holm on his dairy farm. I was talking to my dad one and just then the harsh reality set in after what he said to me.

My dad told me to my face that I would not amount to much. I was shocked that he thought that I wouldn't after all I had done with him. In a lot of ways what he had said to me that has changed my life forever and the way I think about things I want to accomplish. In a lot of ways what he told me that day is still driving me after almost thirty years later after he said it.

I set out after that to prove him wrong, but did it led to the right choices. It did in some aspects of my life, but others could have been better. It was one of the drivers that prompted me to join the U.S. Navy. I learned a lot of things from the military and I also learned a lot of things about myself when I was in the service. It was at that time I begin to wonder if I was really in love with Della and if I had married her for all of the right reasons or even ready to be married. Was I really ready to settle down at that time, but now there was a whole new world opened up to me. I have asked myself that question and many other questions since the divorce. With that whole new world came a lot of new choices for me to make.

It was then the desire to get into business started, and as part of that foundation was a college degree. A degree that took over ten years to finally receive, and a desire to get my real estate license. With that real estate license I am going to get a degree in Computer Drafting and Design. It has meant a lot to me in getting my business degree with an accounting emphasis, and it will mean even to me when I get my degree in Computer Drafting and Design. I do have a desire to go on to get a degree in Project Management then maybe a master's degree in Real Estate Development. I had changed directions and went into business building home decor items.

Success is one step at a time, and in time that success will become real. Hard work will pay off that I am putting into achieve that success. I have been investing, but I still have lots to learn about investing. I have been following a lot of Warren Buffett has to say about investing. It is all about the long term investments. I started off building on my foundation toward that desired dream. Everything in life starts with a good foundation in your life.

Webster Dictionary

Success-n. is

1. favorable result
2. The gaining of wealth, fame, etc.
3. Successful one

Success was making money in the stock market even though the stock market had crashed. It was 2008 the housing crash was taking place and stocks were losing money. It was at that point when I decided to get into the stock market. A quality stock is what I looked for when I was investing my money in stocks and bonds. It was stocks of companies that I had known of for years and trusted.

I also looked at the stocks that had increased the dividends that they paid out. When people were selling I was in the market buying the stocks. I was following what Warren Buffet had to say about the market when I was looking and buying the stocks that I wanted to buy for my portfolio. The success has had its ups and downs though. Many things have changed since that has made it tougher to. Never give-up on your dream no matter how long it takes or tough things can get.

One thing I learned in the U.S. Navy was how import communication can be to things, and how the lack of communication can feed into the start of a lot of rumors. I remember the lack of communication during 9/11 and the need to know was there as things were happening very quickly. The higher up in the navy didn't want to get things wrong if they said something. They also weren't sure was going on, and because that rumors went around the ship, like maybe we were headed back to the Persian Gulf.

It has taught me how import communication can be, because it will put an end to the rumors and guessing that can go in a lot of situations. Communication isn't always the military's strong suit even though the military is built on team work and always being detailed oriented. Team work and being detailed oriented is drilled in our head from the day we set foot in boot camp. The team work and paying attention to detail is re-enforced on a daily basis's by the company commander.

I know I have been guilty of keeping things to myself when I should have been communicating them to the rest of the people I was working with. Later on in my military career I did get better at communicating things that needed to be done, and how they needed to be done. Communication is where success starts in your life, yourself and your mindset is a state of your mind and character. It is the most important up and down the chain of command, and it can spell the difference whether your business is a success or a failure.

If you are in vision what your life what would be if you were out of debt. The vision could be a simple but the end result might lead to you being then you were in debt. The vision I had for my life resulted with me being rich and happy. When I am going to dream it is not going to be a small dream it is going to be big dream. Why should someone dream small if they are going to dream. The bigger the vision the bigger and grander the result and pay off for you it could be, but you have to be willing to face failure to come out a winner in the end.

# Chapter 2

## The mindset

The military also had their way of reinforcing that mindset they wanted you to have and that was through doing a lot of marching, drills and a lot of exercising. Sometimes they would make us do push-ups and set-ups just because they wanted us to do them. It not only reinforced a good mindset, but they used it to build good team work. First off negative thoughts and talk is the fear in your mind telling you that you are not worthy of having more or having that dream you always wanted. Well you need to push through that fear with positive thoughts and that you are worthy of more and that you do love yourself for whom you are. Fear may think they own your thought but fear don't own your thought you do, so take charge of your thought and own your thoughts. Thinking positive about yourself and your surrounding yourself with positive people that will keep you motivated to achieve your dream or goals. You also must love yourself as a whole, and for who you are and be truly passionate about what you are doing with your life because things will get tough.

Love for yourself and being passionate about what you are doing will carry you through those tough times in your life and in your business. The mindset is also about how you feel about yourself and how you care about yourself inward and outward appearance that you present to other people on a daily basis. Does that outward appearance give off a vibe that attracts people or does it repel people from you? Well if it does you need to work on your mindset and love and care for self truly and deeply inside and out. Positive thought first starts with loving and accepting who you are as a person. Shifting your thoughts to ones more positive and believing in those thoughts. You have to believe that you are worthy of more and walking that walk each and every day toward that better life. Make all business and career decisions in alignment with who you really are inside and out.

It is very hard to keep yourself motivated to achieve the kind of success you wish or desire to have. Sometimes I do have those negative thoughts about myself, but it is my desire to succeed that pushes me forward. Those thoughts I had could be harsh thinking that I am a worthless piece of shit and that I don't deserve to be happy. The main reason I do feel like that sometimes is that sometimes I do believe that really no one cares about this one, but I know that isn't true because if you believe in God.

God and the lord and savior truly do care about this one and they always will. Those were even harsher than what my own dad had thought of me. Telling myself that I was worthy, and writing it down that I deserved to be a successful. You will then need to repeat it to yourself on a daily, and that way you reinforce that new and successful mindset you are trying to create on a daily basis's. A strong mindset is what helped me make money in the stock market even though the markets had crashed toward the end of 2008. Knowing the goals I had in mind and what I want to achieving investing. The crash of 2008 anybody that was in the market could make money during that time.

I had started working toward the business degree in the fall of 1997, but I had to put it on hold when I went to sea while I was in the U.S. Navy. The U.S. navy offered classes because there was so many personal wanted to get into the classes. The Navy needed a way to weed out the people because they could only let so many people into the classes. These classes were only general like English, math and maybe some science classes. These classes I had already taken at the local community college. It didn't matter that I had college credits behind me, and taken college classes prior to transferring to the VFA-151. It may have taken me awhile to complete the degree and anything that is worth completing and pursuing to a successful end is worth it. I do have it completed and a few other goals I had set for myself.

In the US Navy, There is one force that has the strongest mindset. It is what makes them the most elite fighting force in the US Military. The first day of boot camp we were shown of movie that was showing us the training that the Navy Seals had to endure. One I couldn't swim and two it would have taken a stronger mindset and even another level of toughness. That is what makes them the toughest and most elite fighting force in the military. They are able to think on their feet and adapt to any given situation because in battle not always every plan goes according to the way that it has been laid out. Being able to adapt to those given situations is also what sets them apart from any other given fighting force.

I pushed through the danger and the fear when that fear is always around me when I had to go up on the flight deck. Just like a support person in a squadron. You have to know what is going on when you go through that hatch, and looking out over your head because an exhaust could be blowing down into the catwalk from a jet turning over head. Now able to step out into the catwalk, and now looking out over the deck to see what jets are turning and which ones are taxing and where to. Eyes always focused on what is around you, and always moving and looking as you suck-up that fear using it to push through it to step out on that deck because someone is counting on you to do your job. You have to have the integrity to make the right decision because someone's life could be depending on that decision you make.

Many decisions I made when I was troubleshooting and final checking the jets, and making the right decision as the jet left the deck. It went off to carry its mission and many other missions. I always had my eyes going on around me. I always keep my eyes going around me, like a support person on deck, a knowing what the competition is doing and who maybe or might being try to enter the market. Many times I had to push through that fear and to carry out the job I was being paid to do because people were counting on me to carry out my job to the best of my training that I had received.

Many days and many missions had been carried out until they had succeeded in achieving and finding the objective of the 9/11 attacks. I was out to sea when the 9/11 attacks went down in New York and Washington DC, and there was a lot and confusion till they finally found out what was going on. The day they went in to get Osama Bin Laden who was behind the 9/11 attack on the United States.

It was a well-planned and a well-executed raid on a compound in Pakistan. It wasn't without its challenges like the helicopter failure, but being able to think on their feet fast. They were able to overcome that failure and complete the mission. That goes back to their training that they received from day one of their Seal training, which is the toughest training that only the cream of the crop completes. That is why you always need a clear picture of what is going on around you in life and in business.

They need that tough mindset because they carry out some of the toughest missions that they are asked to do by the US Government. It is also one thing that sets the military apart as a whole because unlike the Germans in World War 2 who were not allowed to think on their feet and adapt to any given situation, that they are allowed to think on their feet and adapt to that given situation. We called it micro management and it can lead to a failure of the unit and your organization. Being able to let go and letting your people adapt and think on their feet will allow your organization to flourish and could be even greater then you expect.

I worked on my college degree in between working here and there ever since I moved home after had broken up with the girl friend. Finally I quit working and went back to school and stuck with it till I got the degree. I also used that strong mindset to get my business degree with an accounting emphasis. I got my first degree in August of 2011 while I was pursuing a degree in Computer drafting and Design from ITT-Tech.

Wanting more besides my business degree led me into working for a degree in Computer Drafting and Design. It was all part of the business that I started working for since I got out of the military. I want part of a good life and I am working toward that life I want and deserve. I have been set back in working toward that goal in getting my degree because I lost my vehicle. I have not given up on getting that degree and I will go back and get as soon as I can. Strength of mind will help me succeed and get what I want out of life.

The Norwegian people are some of the strongest minded people. They had to be because they lived on some of the most rugged land and places in the North. The snows made for some of the most rugged and tough winters to live in. Along with being the most determined people to succeed in whatever they set their mind out to do. It is what helped them when they set out to discover and settle briefly a brave new world. It led my grandparents to push out of Norway in a desire for a better life and for their descendants to come.

That mindset has paid great dividends for whatever I have set out to do and obtain like getting my business degree. It had also helped me succeed in the military service. It has helped me

succeed in whatever I have set out to do and obtain since I have seen my parents struggle throughout their life. I wanted more and better for my life, and a strong mindset will help me obtain that for my life.

In the military they always told us there was a step by step process that we had to go through when doing our job. It was an analytical process that we had to go through when we did each step toward the job that we were assigned to do. Just like there is a step by step process in building a business structure, and that is knowledge. Once gaining that knowledge that you need and then you need to put that knowledge to work for you. That is what led me to go back college and get my business degree.

It takes a strong mind to execute your vision and for it to be a success. Most people at the first signs of failure would shy away because they hate failure. They think failure is bad because all during your school and college life you are taught that failure is bad. In business failure is how you learn how to be successful and it takes a strong mindset to face failure and stick with it. If you have failed learn from and make the need adjustments and push forward to reach your winning mindset.

# Chapter 3

# Strength of character

I get my strength of character from both of my parents. Both my parents told me to treat people that I met like I would be treated. I have always lived by what they had told me and told me to do. I got scared of me grand-ma and out of being scared I let that lie slid from my mouth. She knew right off that I was lying to her, and being afraid wasn't excess to lie to her. One thing I always tell about my family is that I got caught by my Grand-ma lying to her. I got a spanking from her, but at the time I felt hurt that she had spanked me. Now I realize that I deserved it for lying to my Grand-ma. My Grand-ma was of the old school discipline in how to discipline a child. A good spanking never did me harm it only straightened my bottom out. That lesson I learned from my grandma I still carry with my to this very day.

Strength of character is how you carry yourself on a daily basis with that special something that you carry around with you on a daily basis. It is also about that passion and drive to do what you love to do in your life. Like the mindset strength of character has a lot to do with how you carry yourself on a daily basis's that you are proud of who you are. The discipline that they had taught me I carried with me when I joined the U.S. Navy. It was easy to follow those in the Navy that were pointed over me, because what my parents had taught me as a child. I can say that strength of character came directly from my parents and the example that they set for me. I was instructed to say yes sir or yes ma'am or no sir or no ma'am to those appointed over me. A few people that I had met while I was in the Navy had a hard time with the discipline. It really wasn't that hard to follow the instruction that you were given.

Not everyone has that strength character to make it through like this this one guy who couldn't take what was going on in boot camp. He did have a squabble with another person in the company. I had to escort him to medical hold where he escaped from and returned to the company barracks. He was caught and later processed out of the U.S. Navy. I found the U.S. Navy a good fit for my character and didn't have too many problems making it through boot camp.

The U.S. Navy built ones character through team work, and lots of hard work. There were plenty of times that they re-enforced and made sure in boot camp that you worked as a team because only as a team could you achieve the goals and the mission of the U.S. Navy. If there was one person who had messed up in your company all in that company suffered the consequence of their screw up. That was their way of building and reinforcing that you need to work as a team to get through boot camp and your career in the U.S. Navy. Which is true about life and in business as well, so if you want to make it in business you need to put together a team who will work with you toward that common goal you have set forth for your business.

The character of a Navy Seal has to be a strong that way they can make it through their training. Only the strong of character and select few make it and able to call themselves a Navy Seal. They don't come along every day and that is what makes them special because only the select few make it to the end. The Seal training builds strong men of strong character, body and mind. The Seal training is not for everyone but you still are able to make it in the military.

One's character is what attracts a person to each other. I have never had that it as I call it. That it is the one thing very few people have. It is the sort of thing that makes you want to be around that person and keep coming back to see them. I do go out of my way to talk to them. I never had the problem of someone going out of their way to see me. That is where the mind set and success comes in to play. People are always attracted to someone who is successful or has comeback from failure to be successful.

People's character makes them who they are. Their character defines who they are plus people let themselves be defined in ways they want to be defined. I have let myself be defined as a U.S. Navy veteran, author, and a drafter besides a hard worker.

<u>Webster Dictionary</u>

Character n.

1. Letter or symbol
2. Characteristic
3. Moral nature or strength
4. Reputation
5. Person in a play, novel, etc.
6. (Inf) eccentric person

Part of my character is determination and that is something refined while I was in the U.S. Navy. I get my determination from my parents and Norwegian ancestry. The Vikings were a determined people in life and when it came to building their ships that gave them an advantage, because their ships were fast, over the people that they met in battle. They were highly skilled crafts men as well as great traders.

Your character says a lot how you handle failure. The people with a strong character don't shy away from failure they embrace it, learn from it and move on from it. It makes for a stronger character and mindset if you have failed. Some of the best brightest and richest people in America have failed at business a number of times.

I have met a few people in the Navy who command respect by just their presence and with that came the power that came with his presence. To me that is true power when you have power by just your shear presence. There are very few people who have that ability and character. On the flip side I have met some people who you lose total respect the person but you still respect the uniform that they are wearing. I had a first class in VFA-151 I lost total respect for this person, but I still respected the uniform that he wore. That holds true in many other things in line cause you are not always going to get along with the person who has been appointed over you at the time. It is about be the bigger person inside and out and still being able to get the job done to the best of your ability.

I had put in for almost two weeks leave and he knew I was planning to take the time off because he had signed it. He later came to me and wanted me to pull the leave cheat because it interfered with him planning to take leave during the time I had planned to be on leave. He was retiring from the Navy and I guess he had a job interview lined up during that time.

I didn't pull the leave cheat though but I never went on leave those days either. I would have never been in corrosion if I would have taken the shop supervisor position that was being thrust up on me at the time because our supervisor was getting his orders modified to return to VFA-125. I passed on it because I felt like I wasn't ready to be supervisor right then. They wouldn't say I got black balled from the shop and sent to corrosion but in reality I was blackballed because I made one mistake and passed on the leadership role.

Even though that did happen to me in the Navy I still do the best job that I possible do for the squadron because I still maintained my moral fiber that I was made of. That is the strength of my character that I had inherited from my parents and their parents before them that has been passed down through the generations of my family tree. I have never been hand anything through the generations, but that moral of fiber that makes up the strength of my character. I have earned or worked hard for anything thing I have gotten or received throughout my entire life. That is why it means more to me that way because I know it was earned through blood sweat and tears.

Some people don't care how that get or receive things in their life which is a testament to their moral fiber that makes up their life. To me they have no real moral fiber that makes up their life and they have no pride in their own life. Pride has sometimes stopped me from asking for help though and your there is a difference in caring how you achieve things throughout your life. Strength in character to make one's life better each and every day is a testament to your strength and moral fiber of your character that you are made of. It is not a sign of weakness to ask for help and but it is a matter of what you do in the long run with your life. It is also a reflection of how you care about your life in the long run.

Make that reflection of your life a strong reflection of how much you care about your life in the long run. Does that reflection of your life reflect the picture of your life reflect the picture you want people to see each and every day, and is it one you are proud of people to see each and every day. Be proud of you your and reflect a moral character that you are proud of people to see!

# Bad partners

I thought I had married the perfect women for me at the time, but overtime her bad traits that I did not know about started coming out as time went by. It was only under a given situation that they really started to show through, so it isn't that overtime will tell you all. I found out that Della needed to know and be able to read everything I had said or write to a person. I found this out after she got her own private yahoo account and when I did the same thing she got mad about it. Now she was asking if I had something to hide from her. I also made the mistake of leaving myself logged into yahoo messenger because with that she knew I got some messages.

I gave her the privacy she deserved but I was not afforded that by her. She always made sure she noted who I talked to so she could talk to them as well. She even went as far as hacking my e-mail accounts and threating who I ever talked to. I am so much better off without her and I am doing my own thing. Out of bad partners you learn to be a better and wiser person for it. I never retaliated against her, but I thought of a better way to get even with her and all the other ones who had hurt me. Then that brings me to the other bad partner who had turned on me when I couldn't come to see her.

Stuff had of mine had gotten left behind and I thought my stuff was in the safe keeping of her mom and family. I never thought my stuff that would be gone through by her family and things that were mine would be taken by her family. I came home on leave while I was back east and I had gotten to look around in her mom's bathroom. To my dis-may under the bathroom sink were pictures from a magazine that I had saved long before we were ever married because I liked the pictures and the articles the magazine had in it. I did confront her about it, but she really didn't say much about or really do much to stop them from going through and taking my stuff. Especially if the stuff had any value that they did take, and I did have a few things that did have some use and value.

She had invited me to come and see her for the weekend, and the day I was to go and see her I told her I couldn't because I didn't have the money for gas. She told me it was alright, but then she got mad at me. She wrote me an e-mail telling me how she wasn't worth a tank of gas, and in some ways she was right because I used money to pay for the internet that could been better spent on that tank of gas. What I didn't tell her was I was talking to a gal that I really wanted to get with and was more of what I wanted in my life. I didn't want to ruin that, but I ruined what I could have had on the other side to.

She told me it was fine but that wasn't the truth, and she told me I was like every other guy who had hurt her. She tried a number time to push me away when she had got with other guys, but I was always there for her to pick-up the pieces of her heart when she got hurt. Teri had called me up on the phone for me to help her move, when everyone else had backed out on her. I dropped everything I was doing at the time and spent all weekend with her helping her move. I was always there for her when she needed someone to lean on and to help her.

I need some bookkeeping help so I proposed to hire her. I couldn't afford to pay her much, but I did the best I could to help her. Even though in the end it got me in trouble with the state. I also helped her fix other people mistakes that they had done to her stuff like making her bed more stable to sleep in. After all I done for her because I knew she needed the help, and I even offered to let her move in with me that way she would have a place to stay while she got on her feet job wise. I always tried to be there for her and never turned my back on her but in the end she turned on me. This will make success that much sweeter in the end for me, and they will not share in that success.

Bad partners could also be bad co-workers that like to cause friction between other co-workers. Case in point while working one they decided to ask me if john was sweet on Jane, and I said no, I wasn't sweet on her. No I don't want to go out with her and I know she wouldn't go out with me any way. Even at that I still decide to help her out with a few things and set her up with some people that could help get what she was looking for. I should have never said, Jane to a shy to Jason but I don't think it was so a shying as it was that Jane wanted to help him out. That was never said and I was confronted the next day by Jason who said I was talking shit about him and Jane. There was words that should have never been said when he confronted me about what I had said on Friday afternoon.

I am not the best of partners either because whatever I attempt to do is done from a base of weakness. When doing something from a base of weakness means whatever I am attempting to do is going to be a failure. I still attempt to do a lot with few resources to make it profitable success. That is the good heart in me pushing to help people on few resources to my name. Smaller steps from a stronger foundation and getting that stronger foundation in place will make you a better partner.

# Good Partners

A good partner does what he is going to do from a base of strength, and with the resources to see it through to profitability. They help you become a success and they work with you. They also give you the privacy you deserve as well. I would never get to know my mom again before she passed away over a year ago. I also was able to get to know my nieces since then as well which has been very nice. I would have not gotten to know them again if I was still with the ex's because I would have spent all of my time with them.

Me being a naval veteran a partner would most have had to be trust worthy, honorable and posse integrity. Integrity was explained to me by Commanding Officer of VFA-151 as doing the right thing when nobody is looking at you. I think in a lot of ways family like my nieces and even my ex-sister-in-law would make excellent partners in my business and in the empire that I am building. There is some family that would not make good partners though, and those people have already shown there true colors, since my mom's passing away. The settlement of her estate has left a bitter pill with me and a couple members of my family.

I think my two sons, Lars and James, would make excellent business partners as well, but here again I cannot stand their mother though. She has shown her true colors many times and can't be trusted at all. If it wasn't for their mother I would already be working with and mentoring them in my business. I do need to get it started though before it is too late to get it started even though I can't stand their mother or trust her.

Success will be the sweetest of revenge against those that would not help me and have turned their back on me over the years. I have known people who had looked out after me after I had gotten dumb and helped me get back to the ship where I would be safe. Those people are a true partner and a shipmate because we always looked out for one of our own. For on the ship in a time of need or disaster your shipmate is therefore the only one there that you can count on in those times of need or disaster.

I wish I had partners now like I had in the navy, because I would have gotten a lot of my goals accomplished and plus I would already be very successful now. Sometimes I know they would get mad at for some of the things I did but even after that they still look after me. They would make sure I made it home, which was the ship, safely and I did some crazy things that did put my safety at risk. It wasn't so much that they cared about me. It was more about that they did want to see me get hurt because of my recklessness. My model for a good business team and partners would be what it was like in the Navy.

Good partners and good co-workers would have never looked to cause friction between other co-workers as they did that week. John should have been a good partner and co-worker and had handled it a lot differently and also what was said should have been so there was no misunderstanding or misinterpretation by those two. Needless to say it has made it a very rough place to work now. Always be the good partner and co-worker and say nothing about any other co-worker.

# Partners

Partners are like a marriage they can be either good or bad, and a partnership is what you make it into. For every bad partner you ever had in your life there just may be a good partner right around the corner. Those good partners would have been overlooked if it weren't for the bad partners I have had in my life. I am being the best partner I can be to attract the best of partners to me.

It is tough because some of the best people I really think and family are a long ways from me. It is hard to carry on a long distance partnership and even a relationship that is long ways a part from you. I am trying to manage a long distance relationship now and trying to juggle a long distance business relationship along with trying to help her get her own business up and running. Getting her own business up and going will help her get through her recovery a lot better after the surgery. It just makes it more of a challenge but it can be done if you just work at it. You never know it might just be a winning relationship that could make you winners in the end.

A partnership agreement can protect you and your assets, because under a limited liability agreement your liability is limited to what each partner puts into the partnership. A partnership agreement is also like a marriage licenses, and now you are joined together under the agreement. That is why you really need to know and trust the person you are entering into the partnership agreement with. Once you have a partnership agreement in place you are partners with that person until the partnership is dissolved which is easier and less expensive than getting out of a bad marriage.

Nobody is going to get anywhere business by themselves plus nobody can run a successful business by themselves. Partners are a key part to running and scaling a successful business. The partners have to be the right fit for the business to grow and scale to the next level and beyond. The partners and employees also must have complete buy in on the vision of the business for it to be successful. The vision of the business is what the business is and a plan of where the business is going and how it is to get to those goals setup in the business plan.

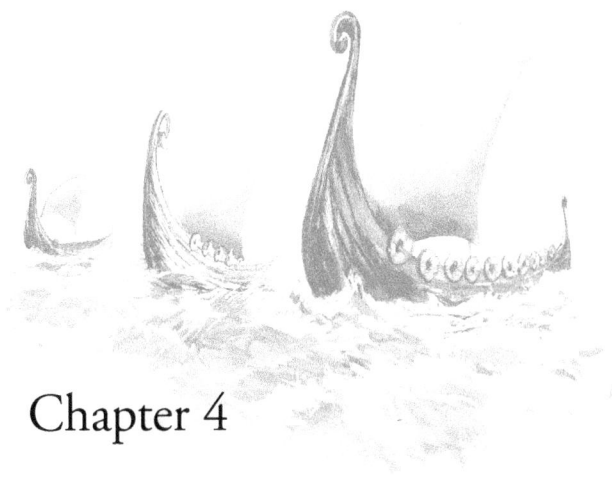

# Chapter 4

## Strength of brand

I didn't think of mowing lawns as a business even though I was working for myself. I wasn't even a brand, so you could say I was a commodity. It was more of a way to make money that I spent on stuff that really added no value to my life. The lawn mowing business started with Mr. and Mrs. Christenson, who worked with my dad on the railroad, mowing their lawn after I got out of school.

Mowing lawns grew one lawn after another and it kept growing in the years to come. I also probably forgot lawns that I was mowing because my organizational skills lacked a lot. Organizational skills are a very big part of running a successful business. Weather played a lot into me missing mowing a lawn, sometimes I didn't mow because it was too hot out. I remember my mom got on to me for that, and told me that I need to keep what I had said I was going to do.

I still mowed lawns now and then but nothing like I had in the tears prior. When my dad got more actively involved with the lawn mowing business, because of a deal he worked out with Mr. Lowell. The owners of the motel were located in New Plymouth, but I made the mistake of even talking to them, which I should have left to him to deal with. It was after that I decided to walk away from mowing lawns all together.

Prior to that and if I would have known what I had learned later on the lawn mowing could have been more than just a job. It may have never been a brand but it could have been more around the community because I was in demand to mow people's lawn for them. I was doing a job or business thus has become a crowded business and hard to differentiate yourself out from your competitor. The making of a successful brand is being able to differentiate yourself from your competitors in the business. That is why when I tried to start mowing lawns again that my business didn't go anywhere. I tried hard to make it successful but still wasn't enough because of way to much competition.

If I had have known things earlier, and had parents that knew more about how to own and operate a business the way it should have been ran. Then it may have proven to be a total different outcome, and it might have proven to be a more successful business then it was.

# My next project

I graduated from New Plymouth High School, and had attended some college at Treasure Valley Community College. That I put to work when I set-up pins for calves for a living. Working for and with Dave Holm I started to buy a calf when I could afford to buy one. Meanwhile, I was purchasing the equipment that I needed to raise them with. The calves that I purchased were cross breed between Hereford and Holstein, a black bawlie, they were called.

I branded my calves the way they had for years with a fire and branding irons. The branding irons that were heated in a fire like the old west cattle drives. I made the fire in a central part of the carrel that held the calves that I wanted to brand. Throwing, holding the calves down, one by one, I put the iron to their hide which I put my mark up on them. That brand was my mark up the hips of the cattle and I could put the same mark that showed who owned the cattle and the horses.

I had found an accounting book that I was keeping track of the cost and the expense that I was accruing in connection with the business. About the end of the year I would sell part of the calves that I was rising to pay my taxes with. I did need a more sustainable source for the cattle, and that is why I acquired a heifer calf to breed. Later I went into the U.S.

Navy and I was forced to sell all of the animals that I had but one which I found out the ex-wife sold before moving to Washington state. That was the downside of me going into the U.S. Navy even though I had planned to carry on raising the calves.

I intended to name my business the Crooked River Ranch after the ranch in the movie "The Outlaw Josey Wales". It was a ranch that Josey Wales moved to after he wouldn't lay down his weapons to the Union Army and they, the United States Government, declared him an outlaw, but while I was in the service I was informed that there already a Crooked River Ranch in Oregon. A person who was in navy boot camp with me, he was from SW part of Oregon. I had my branding iron already created for the ranch, but since then I no longer have those branding irons.

The US Navy Seals are one the most elite and prestigious brands in the US Military. Their training is the toughest to get through and very few make it through that training. It is not about being the strongest and able to lift the most weight to get through the training. Only the toughest physically, and strong mentally able in the end able to earn the seal trident and able to call themselves a Navy Seal. The Navy Seals came into being in the 1960's when President Kennedy recognized a need for a small, and elite force to carry out mission that the Gov't need done by a small and elite force. Seal stands for Sea, Air and Land, and that's the way they operate.

They were a force that was not very well known about unless you were in the US military. The operated in the shadows, secretive and close net community, and that is why they were able to carry out their best work. The training is so tough which helps to develop the tough mindset that they will need to carry out the tough missions they are called upon to perform for the US Gov't. One the toughest missions they had to perform was the raid on a compound in Pakistan that got Osama Bin Laden. It made them a very recognizable force worldwide, but they would rather operate in the shadows because that is when they do their best work.

In this era of the internet and the information age, and the information on the internet moves fast. Something's on the internet are very informative and something's are not so much. The Seal training and standards are tough because the missions they have to carry out are the toughest and the most dangerous. The is why only the cream of the crop get to call themselves a Navy Seal, but read some articles that say the Seals should reflect more of society as a whole.

In order to accomplish that I would think they would have to modify their training, lower their standards, and how would that reflect on the Seal brand. The brand is not for everyone and they are not everything to everyone. Their training is tough for a reason because it weeds out the weak minded and weak of heart. That way only the best get to be part of the Seal brand. That is what makes the Seals an elite fighting force.

The information has forced a lot of brands to either adapt or change their business model to accommodate the information age, and if they don't then they will more and likely have to close the doors on the business.

# Status symbol

There is some people who love to have the biggest and the largest of cars they could get. There are a lot of people that did when gas was really cheap in the 70's. The streets don't work very well and aren't wide enough for those cars though. I have almost got in an accident because the cars swing wide and over into the next lane. Cars swinging wide into other lanes can cause an accident because side roads are too small and was created to accommodate only small cars. I have come close to hitting a few of those vehicles to.

I am not into those kinds of things though. I am not a flashy person who has to call attention to himself. My brand is not going to be built on those kinds of things. I am a simple person raised with simple values. A status symbol does work for some people though. A status symbol doesn't make a brand being true to yourself is what makes a brand.

# My parent's advice

My parents taught me a lot of things. Mostly how to work hard for others, but he did show me a few things about being a carpenter and the carpentry business. Following their example in a lot of ways and being honest to myself. I have never tried to be everything to all people, because that isn't possible to do. My dad never tried to be all things to all people because knew that wasn't possible. I have known people that have tried to be everything to everyone. Being honest to yourself means sticking by your guns when things get tough for you. Things have gotten tough for me a lot of times.

My mom made sure I was brought up in the church, and to respect other people. I followed what I was taught in the church and lived my life in the way I was taught in church. She told me that I should treat people the way that I would like to be treated, and that is to be treated with respect. That is the one thing that she made sure that I always would remember and to put in to practice in my life.

Webster Dictionary

Brand n.

1. Burning stick
2. Owner's mark burned into cattle
3. Stigma
4. Make or kind–v. mark with a brand

# The Brand

A brand has meaning and it has real value. Value and real meaning behind brand is what gives the brand real value. A fake or knock off brand may have meaning but it lacks one and that is real value. When the brand is sold to another company does it still retain that same value or the meaning that it had before it was sold. Do the new owners have the same passion for the business that you had as owner before you sold it.

This brand starts with the company's core values of the business which are integrity, courage and commitment. They are some of the values I learned while in the United States Navy. I carried them with me into my civilian life and into my business life. I have put one piece at a time, and I am learning the skills from my college classes to bring the dream I am trying to build alive. Building houses and building is the main part of my business that I am going to build. I am going to college to get a degree in designing building and houses. I want to work on getting a degree in project management.

The dream is starting with the Olsen Organization. The building of home décor of medieval design and Viking design along with western items. I would like to get back into raising calves for sale and use for personal and in a restaurant and grill. I got a brand to use on calves and horses. It would be a part of a dance club that would serve no beer or liquor. It would be about the dancing that would showcase a lot of local talent from around the valley. The building of businesses I am passionate about running and operating. Business for myself and my loved ones is my purpose in this life after I got out of the service.

That is only a small part of the overall dream that I want to build for myself and my ancestors. The buildings that I build will carry my ancestor's surname. It will be enhanced by the internet in this era of the information age. I have been making my presence felt already via the company website, facebook and twitter.

# Chapter 5

## Strength of network

The strength of network is how I was adding mowing jobs to what I was doing. The people I was mowing lawns for knew my parents, and some of them belonged to the same clubs as my mom did. My mom's friends were referring me to mow the lawn of who ever needed their lawns mowed. To me that proved how strong the network was in helping me gain new lawns to mow. They were also people who attended the same church that we attended. It also proved to me how important a strong network can be in getting places you want to go in life.

I used my connection and working connection to acquire the calves that I was raising for my business. He helped me pick out the calves that I purchased from him. I also used the network to help me when I had a problem in raising my calves, and when it came time to sell the calves at the stock yard. The calves I was most interested was the Holstein and Hereford cross, a black bawlie, that I bought from him.

Webster Dictionary

Network n.

1. Arrangement of wires or threads as in a net
2. System of roads, computers, etc.
3. Chain of radio or TV stations-v.

Network v.

1. To form into a network
2. Develop business, etc. contacts

A network is made up of people who won't work against you and wants to partner with you on the project. They are a person who will work with to achieve that goal or dream but I had neither one while I was in the military or married. A network is one that will help you build a dream and it is also one that will help you when times get tough, because sometimes you do hit those rough patches in one's life. I have had my share of down days, but I know I can get through those tough times because of my strength of character and my mindset.

Part of that network can be social media because with it things can move faster and reach a wider group of people in a very short time. They can also give you feed back in a very short time as well. Feedback can help you build a better network, and it can also help you build a better product. A better product or products will help you build a better brand. A better and strong brand is good. Reaching more people can be good for your business and your brand. The information move on the internet moves for good or bad at the speed of you pushing enter on your key board. That is why you have to sort through the information that you do find on the internet, because there is so much information on the net in this information age.

It is good to set-up a partnership with someone to protect both parties in the network. That way both members in the partnerships know where they stand within the partnership. It also has great tax advantages for both members of the partnership. I had plans to set-up a partnership with my nieces that way we would both be protected and have great tax advantages that go along with being in a partnership. I feel that need to make those people around me there life better as I make my life better and fulfill the dream that I have for my life. I want people's lives to be better around me because I know how I hate living paycheck to paycheck. I have lived that way my entire life and it isn't a fun feeling either. Lifting someone else's life is a very uplifting feeling and it also can make for a stronger and better network.

Think of your network as a phone line the feeds into one common line and as part of that network you should have a mentor/ coach. The mentor/ coach will keep you on the path and they will also hold you accountable if you miss a step toward reaching your goal. Surround yourself with people that have a common vision, and that are high energy people. People who have things in common and can relate to you are more fun to be around. People that will lift you up, get you excited about life. Keep you going and make you a stronger person. They can also help you expand, evolve, and help you innovate your business with each coming new trends but changing with each new upcoming trend can be very expensive. Choose wisely when to evolve and innovate.

# Chapter 6

# Communication

Communication also means sharing what your brand is and also what your brand stands for. A great brand needs to communicate that to all the members of the businesses cause all the people need to be onboard completely with the brand and there vision for it to be successful business.

Communication means sharing information throughout all employees of the business and not holding back communication that would allow you to get the job done in a timely manner.

Communication should also be allowed to be free flowing from top to bottom and also from the bottom to the top. Not allowing for that information to be free flowing could cause jobs not to get done in a timely manner. The lack of the problem of no communication of what needs to be done can cause the job not to be done in a timely manner or it also can cause the job to be not done right. The job I currently have has a lack of communication and it is to the point where they will not allow that free flowing communication to take place. Plus you also need that great vision in place. You also need to be able to communicate that vision to all members of the business.

People need to know what needs to, how and when it should be done. They also need to know what is to be accomplished that work day. They should also know what is expected of them each and every day. The lack of communication can be very costly and expensive in the long run. It also can cause you to waste man power and material, and in today's economy is very expensive now due to inflation.

The business also needs to change and innovate as the society and times dictate. Those innovations need to be dictated to all people throughout all the businesses if you have more than one business. A business that is able to innovate all time as times change has a great long term prospects. The art of communication is the key to all great businesses being able to get where they need to be and go where they need to go in the space there in. business is about offering a product that fulfills the persons wants or needs. That is why you also need to communicate with your customers all of the time. That way you can get a sense of what products they are looking for.

Your actions speak louder than anything you can ever say. If you say you are going to do something than follow with what you said you are going to do. Do what you say with a plan though. Get input from partners, co-workers, employees, and customers about the project. A doer is a great example for one's business and the brand you are building. Be that great example for the business and the brand. It is how I look at friends, people I meet and all those people I meet in my daily life.

# Are You a Communicator?

If you do want to be a success you have to learn to be a great communicator to get your point across to the people. Ronald Reagan was dubbed the great communicator as President of the United States in the 80's. Steve Jobs was another great communicator who as CEO led Apple to the great heights that the company is enjoying today. Upon his death he has left behind some pretty big shoes to fill by the next CEO that has taken over the helm of the Apple Company.

As The great communicator, President Reagan was able to achieve great things in his eight years as office. He was most noted for his strong stance against the unions, and his firing of all the Air Traffic Controllers got rid of the Air Traffic Controller union. He also supported anti-communists groups around the world in an effort to keep the spread of communism from spreading throughout the world.

He advocated supply side economics polices that were, dubbed "Reaganomics", to control the money supply to reduce inflation and thus spurring economic growth by reducing tax rates, Government regulation of the economy and certain types of Government spending. He also advocated a massive military build-up in which President Reagan wanted to build a 600 ship U.S. Navy. Which most of his policies and thing he had done for the military has been dismantled since them by the Presidents who succeeded after him.

I have been learning to be a better communicator since I have went back to college and as part of the better communication is to be better prepared with the speech. Being prepared also means having the answers for any questions that may be asked of you or may come up as part of your speech or the discussion. It was a big part of my final college classes that I was taking.

It is just like when you enter into a business deal with investor or negations for that piece of real estate you are looking to purchase. Always be prepared for any questions or those unexpected things that might come up during the talks can help you get the best price possible for that land. Being a great communicator can help you persuaded the other side and that is what negations is all about. Persuasion of the other side is the key to negations.

Alexander the Great is another example of a great communicator and a person being able to persuade people to follow him on his conquest of the world. His journeys were long and hard and not the most easy of journeys and battles. He was also prepared down to the littlest of details and prepared for any given situation that may arise during the battles that he commanded. Channel your inner Alexander the Great or Ronald Reagan and be the greatest communicator and prepared for any given situation. Along with being a great communicator are you a great and willing listener to those that you have surround yourself with.

# A Great Listener

Sometimes it may take a while to find those people to surround yourself with because you only want the best talent around you. Like they always, hire slow but fire fast. A business owner you need to surround yourself with the best people for their varying strengths that compliment you and those that are around you. Why would you surround yourself with the best people and varying strengths if you are going to be stubborn and really unwilling to listen to those that are around you.

Part of building a good and strong brand is leveraging and utilizing those talents and strengths of those that you have surround yourself with. It is not a weakness to listen to another person. It is a sign of a great leader if you do listen to their advice and taking their advice in hand. Then acting and utilizing that advice that you have received from those advisors and workers around you.

I used to think it was a weakness to listen and take someone's advice under advisement. I was made to think I was wispy washy if I changed my mind when I had first made my mind up to do something or had given an order to those around me to do something. I was looked down up on by those that were my superiors that were over when I often would change my mind.

Now I know it is alright to change my mind and to change course because sometimes that change in course is for the better. I have been the person that was in flexible and didn't want to listen to other people's advice and sometimes it can be very costly and time consuming if you don't listen to those other people to. We had a five minute repair job to do at night, but being the way I was I turned it into an all-night repair job. It took us several tries to get the job done right, but by the time I left the Navy I don't think we ever got any of them truly repaired right.

I have been watching a movie about "Arn: A Knights Templar" and it has made me realize how
arrogant and stubborn some leaders can be. Being so arrogant and stubborn to the point you

won't listen to peoples advice of those around you. It cost them in the end because he was so arrogant not to listen to those people around him. That is what got all the Knights Templar killed in the Holy Land.

It also taught me one other good thing that is a good battle field commander should and be willing to tell the overall person in to fall back and to regroup or change direction if necessary when it comes to doing a job right the first time. It is too costly to have to do the job over and over again, so that is why you want to always do it right the first time. Take their advice under advisement and make the best decision possible. Stick with that decision you made, but be flexible enough to change course as the needed for when change in a task is called for. Sometimes change of course are forced to as the change in circumstances dictates.

# Vision

The vision of the business is what the business is and where the business is going. Also how the business will get to where it is going. It is the business plan for the business for at least five years of the business. It also sets the goals for the business long term. Those goals should be real and realistic in nature but also dreams that are big. The dreams should not be small ones because why else would you have went into business for yourself and your partners and in your network. Everyone needs great partners and network in order to build a great business as no one person can carry out everything for the business to grow and scale up.

That takes a great vision and great communication to all people in your business each and every day. Communication is the key to a great business. All members of the business have to buy into the vison of the business in order to get it where it is going, and there for it to be able to scale up each time. The vision also needs to take in to account the need to innovate and change as the times and society evolves. Innovation and being able to evolve are keys to the long term growth and being able to scale up your business to the next level. The vision is about fulfilling the needs of that customer.

# Chapter 7

## The little things

The little things can help enhance your strength of brand. The little things are what make for a good foundation. A good foundation is what everything is built up on. It is like a house or a skyscraper is built on a good strong foundation and it there to absorb and also support the structures that it is built upon the foundation. There also has to be a great foundation to that relationship and friendship and if not it will just fall a part in a short time it will crumble. A relationship and even a friendship that is built upon to many expectations or better yet an illusion will fail and leave people hurt and broken hearted in the end. That is why a foundation for structure, relationship and friendship has to be strong and sound because it serves several purposes as part of the overall building structure, relationship and friendship. That is why every load of concrete is tested by the building inspector before it goes into the structure's foundation.

Working in the aircraft community in the U.S. Navy taught me how important the littlest of details can mean the difference between a successful mission and even death and lose of aircraft. That is why paying attention to detail is drilled into your head from day one. I have seen it happen to some finest pilots while I was in the service. If it was proven to be your fault it could cost you if you found guilty by court martial. The penalty for being found guilty could mean you could be spending time in a jail cell.

I told a guy that I worked with at Nampa-Meridian Dutch Co. that if you take pride in the little things of the job that you are doing. Then you take pride in how the overall job is going to come out. I was washing one of their pick-ups that were covered in dust and mud. They use these pick-ups to run up and down the ditch banks with in there water district. Taking pride in your work also shows your supervisor and people that you care about the work you are doing and doing it right the first time. I may have not had passion for the job I was doing but I still took pride in doing the best I could for them

The people that had lived in the barracks before the group I was with cleaned and waxed the decks. The barracks failed that week's inspection and because that were made to clean the barracks that evening. One thing as crew leader I always got the person that was in charge of regiment to do a pre inspection. That way we didn't miss anything before the real inspection took place. I failed to do that, and the group I was with paid the price for the failed inspection.

Speaking of having to do a job over there was this time in the Navy that I had to do a job over again after another crew messed the job up. We had to strip an entire floor to get rid of the wax build-up along the base board, because the shipmates who lived in the barracks didn't care about doing the job right. It was not the last time we had to clean someone else's job for them. Me, and some other shipmates had to strip the deck, because wax had yellowed, due to wax build-up and re-wax the deck.

That is why I guess I am slow on the job because I want to do it right, but they want it done fast. They not only want it done fast but they want it done right the first time. To me fast and right don't go well in the same sentences. I know there are a lot of fast paced jobs out there to. Building a structure can be a very fast paced job to; because the foundation does require a fast pace before it sets up. You have to take time to work it with a vibrator, and trowels. Vibrating the concrete helps work the air out of it a work the rocks in the concrete and smoothing out the top of it. That way the walls have a smooth surface to be seeded upon. An uneven surface can make for uneven walls and make the walls so they are not true and square.

I have done concrete work for a dairy farmer, who didn't care too much how the job turned out,

but we still tried to smooth it out even though it was just to keep cows in the free stall barns. The driveway though he had a different purpose for it so he wanted it to be smooth and the rocks worked into the concrete. It was long and hard work but in the end it was all worth it.

Webster Dictionary

Foundation n.

1. Establishment or basis
2. Base of a wall, house, etc.
3. Philanthropic fund or institution

One mis-step can mean the difference between success and failure and also timing sometimes can mean everything if you are trying to invest in stocks and bonds, and real estate. Sometimes the best deals only come around once and if you're not ready to invest then you already lost out on the opportunity.

In Battle the littlest of things missed can make the difference of you are coming out of the battle dead or alive. Battle is like a chess game move and countering your opponents move and anticipating your opponent's moves. That means planning your moves in the battle down to the littlest of details, and then revaluating your opponent's moves during the battle. You need to be able to adjust your moves to counter your opponent's moves on the battle field that is business. You need to be able to pay close attention to the small details, because the sum of all the small details can make a big and tremendous difference in consequences. It can also cost your business a lot of money in the long run. That is why it is crucial to pay attention to the smallest of details when making out your detailed plans.

# Chapter 8

## My vision

My vision for my life and business life started with a picture vision board. I cut out pictures representing the parts of how I would like the life to look like as Norwegian Fjord and paint horses, Red Angus cows, American and Norwegian cash, stocks and bonds. Looking at the pictures as I write out how the vision fits together also how it looks like. My own store front where I design and build home décor items out of real wood and not out of particle board. I have built and designed barn doors, a bed, television cabinets, different wood boxes, shields, tables. It is a place where we live and sell the items in different part of the United States and Europe, such as Idaho, Hawaii, Norway and Denmark.

Owning different places as rentals in the areas I would like to operate. Owning different businesses in different sectors in in the places I would like to be in. Picturing how I would like to be in time and owning my own way in how to get around. It is a road map or a business plan of how your business is to be, how to get there, and where the business is head to in the long term. You can also set goals for different stages of the business that you would like to obtain over time as the business grows and you fulfill how that vision that you would like to have. Adding pictures to the picture vision as I see how the vision fits together. Taking in account about what I had learned over the years also about what I enjoyed over years and had experienced in n my life.

Details of the business matters, as you make the details out for your business. You can Tweak those details to your vision of your business plan periodically. Doing what you love to do is not a job. It is also something you will love to do on a daily bases. It will make your life worth living on a daily bases. Do something you enjoy cause you will love doing it on a daily bases.

# Chapter 9

## A week in my life

I am an early morning riser, and my day begins by reading through the main sections of USA today, the Norway Post, Irish times, Ice News, and the Jersey Evening Post. Taking a mile walk after I turned on the today show and making a pot of coffee. A relaxing walk prepares me for the work ahead of me that day. Having got ready I head to work at 8:45, and having arrived at work. I check on how the stock market is doing that day. Once ready I went about my days work.

Monday 2 July 2012

0900 I worked on my photo shop class assignment for my photo shop class at ITT-Tech Institute to work on class work for my Tuesday class at 6 pm. The room I decided to design had a Medi-eval theme to it. It is a class that will help me prepare for life after college.

1200 Made a phone call about a job in Payette who was looking for a part time CAD-Tech. Went back to work on my homework for my Photo Shop class.

1 pm working on that big picture vision for the business.

1:30 pm Called USAA to talk to a financial advisor about my portfolio I hold with them. Talking over another financial matter with them that could help me grow my money and pay off my debts that I owe. I also talked to them about some investment opportunities and some real estate investments that were out there.

Tuesday 3 July 2012

0900 Worked on homework for 3D/S max CAD class. I have thought about taking the buildings that I had designed in my CAD classes, and building them in New Plymouth. It will look great with a mixed building that I had designed in my Architecture class. I have also thought about pushing them higher and making the buildings bigger. I have picked out the piece of ground that I would love to build the buildings on. I am thinking how New Plymouth can be more that it is right now.

1200 I drove to New Plymouth and helped Martina with her homework. I continued to work on my homework, and showed her what I had been working on in my CAD class.

1 pm Adds to and adjusts that big picture by investing in the stock market.

1:15 pm Talk to USAA stock advisor about my portfolio goals. I had been in mutual funds with Wells Fargo so I didn't want to invest in them. They had advised me into investing into the funds. I kept the way I was investing.

Wednesday 4 July 2012

0900 called different dealerships that had cars for sale. I did set-up to look at a car. I worked on homework for my CAD class.

1200 look at more dealerships for a car and made a phone call to my niece Martina for help cause I was in need of a ride to get to my college classes. I also filled her in on what was going on with my car, but I had overheated the motor and warped the head so then it would leak anti-freeze between the engine block and the head. Mixing it with my oil, and when that happens you have to replace the motor.

Thursday 5 July 2012

0900 Left with my niece Martina to go look at the car I had decided on, but I was informed that the car I was to look at had an engine problem. I looked at a different car, but didn't get that car.

It took me most all day and tried different ways to get the car but in the end it still didn't work out in my favor.

Friday 6 July 2012

0900 I left for school so I could work on homework that I needed to get done for the class I had that night. I also needed to get the homework for the class I had missed the night before.

1:00 pm I went to Burger King for lunch. Once I finished my lunch I got back to work on my homework for my 3D/S Max drafting design class.

1:30 pm sell stocks and buy other stocks for my portfolio. Investing in stocks that I know and trust for the long term.

The weekend

It has been a trying quarter that has been added to with the car problems that I am now going through. I have been working on homework for my classes that I have this week, but once again I was looking for a car. I am hoping that I can find a car quickly because I am missing out on my capstone class because I really wanted to graduate. My instructor, Kay Jones, Really wanted me to graduate and see tried her hardest to find a way to get me to my classes.

It was just not to be though, and I ended up dropping the entire quarter. I would love to get that off of my mind and concentrate on finding a job and back on to my homework. I would love for things to get back to normal. I talked to my sister about planning a book release party for the book I had just released. Some of the days the work is different from other days, and I never knew what challenge would come my way, but I dealt with those challenges head on day by day. Challenges are always a part of one's life.

# Chapter 10

## Learning from your mistakes

Mistakes are the best teachers and the greatest way to learn. Mistakes being failure is life's teacher but in school failure is a bad thing. Failure in school means you failed the class. Failure in the world of business means you learn from it and move to the next remembering your failures you learned from. Failure in real life is one of the greatest teachers in our life, but you won't learn that from the school system. My biggest mistake was getting deep into debt in other wards over extending myself money wise even when I was married. I have made that money mistake more than once. I have tried not to make the mistake once more but sometimes it is very hard not to once more.

Fear of failing is the one thing that can hold you back from learning what you need to know, so don't be afraid to fail cause everyone fails in their life. Fear is being afraid of the unknown. Some fear is a good thing in your everyday life. So don't let fear hold you back from the goals in your life and in business. That is why I have read and learned more about money, also that is why I have also been investing part of my earnings each month.

I also learned more about investing along the way, but I still have lots more to learn about investing. Can you really learn everything about investing? That is why I have been investing in stocks of companies that I know and steered clear of stock funds as I had lost greatly on those funds. I have made money on a couple select funds such as short term bond fund and a precious gold fund. With that in mind I have been investing for the long term.

Learning who are great partners and bad partners in your life and even in your business life cause one person can't do everything for a successful life or even a successful business life. It takes partners to scale a successful business to greatness. Communication among partners and employees is also a key element of a successful business cause not much can be accomplished without lots of communication through the entire business. Communication is also a healthy part of your life. Fear and failure will always be part of life. Fear also lets you know you are alive to.

Government always has a way of setting your business back or even causing it to fail if you don't pay attention to your business and what the government is doing. It is the one key player in your business life. It can also cause you many mistakes along the way, but learn from them and move on from them. Taxes are another thing that can cause you to make a big mistake even if you are not the one that does your taxes. I had that happen to me once, and it was a little expensive to. So pay attention to whoever does your taxes for you. I later learned what had happened from another tax person what had happened when I had my taxes done the following year.

Mistakes and failure can come in many forms, shapes and sizes and also those mistakes and failures can happen to you when you are down and least expecting things to happen to you. Pay attention all of the time and always know what your partners and what your employees are doing all of the time. Communicate with them all, and get updates from them about what they are doing and any projects they have going on. Be a leader and take ownership of those failures learn from them and move forward from those failures. Don't be a bad leader and pass the buck off on to your partners or employees. Key parts of the business of the business you truly need to pay attention to in your business or businesses. Always know your numbers when it comes to your business. Know what those numbers tell you about how your business is doing.

# Chapter 11

# Financial statement

A financial statement is a picture of your overall financial health. Learning how to interpret and how to read what your financial statement is telling you will help you reach your financial goals. The biggest key to building a strong financial statement is that you need accurate and vital financial information in a timely manner. There is so much information out to be collected and sorted through, but the key is you need to sort through all of that information in a timely manner cause sometimes time can be your enemy. This is where a good financial advisor would be very handy who could help you with the best financial advice they have. Leveraging their time and knowledge can help you toward your financial goals of being wealthy. Building a stronger financial statement and credit history should go hand in hand cause they just as equally important.

I have leveraged my time and wrote my life story which was an expense, but soon that could pay off in royalties and copyrights to my book which will be an asset once it is published. The reason for me writing my life began as way for me to write out the lessons I have learned over the years. It has been a life that has seen its ups and downs along with its challenges that I had to face over the years. I wrote about my dream I had for my life, and that dream lead me to writing this book on finance.

I had leveraged my time, knowledge and things I had learned in my journey in learning and improving my own overall financial picture. This book will also add to my assets once it is published. Those intellectual copyrights will be owned and protected by a business entity. It also started with leveraging my time and learning about investing which was an expense, but that helped me with my investing for value which turned it into an asset. I have seen my financial picture suffer its setbacks, but learning from those setbacks can help you make better and wiser financial decisions on down the road. I will use those lessons I had learned to improve my financial statement and overall financial picture.

# Financial statement

My financial looks and will look like this.

| Exwpenses | Assets |
|---|---|
| normal expenses | investment portfolio |
| time | My life's book |
| knowledge | This book on finance |
| learning | savings |
| | land |
| | cash |

The learning never ends or stops cause there is always something to learn each and every day, so you can tap into and find that inner financial guru that is in each of us. The better you look asset to debt ratio then the better chances it is you are going to get that bank loan.

# Chapter 12

## Olsen Hidden Ranch, El Paso, TX

I had looked at a few places over the years like the one where my mom and dad lived at in New Plymouth, ID. I had also looked at a place in Virgina Beach, VA. I have always wanted to own my own place where I would live out my life at. I have also looked at a few different places where I would like to own real estate at in the world. I read in local newspaper that there was foreclosed property for sale in El Paso, TX. I did some research on the internet on property that was for sale. I thought long and hard about the property that was for sale in El Paso, TX. I had to believe the company I was dealing with was real and that I wasn't getting taken by them. I saw the property as a good investment, but I kept on looking for that one right piece of property.

Once I had finally found that right piece of property. I downloaded and printed out the land property agreement to purchase a piece of ground in the El Paso, TX area. I didn't have any negotiations with the owner of the property. I had a few ideas for the property while looking at several magazines that contained blue prints of different houses. I did decide on a house that I would love to build on the land.

Choosing a building site means everything to your overall comfort in the house. There should be no surprises when you move into the house unlike a home that was built in Rexburg, ID. It was a five bedroom house that was priced at $180,000.00 and Jeff and his wife thought it was a steal at that price. The snakes released a foul smelly musk into the water. They said they could hear noises in the walls of the house. Mr. Sessions killed

42 snakes in one day. They found out their surprise that the house was infested with thousands of Garter Snakes.

It was noted in the documents that Jeff had thought of it as a way for the previous owners to get out of the contract and in the end they walked away from the house themselves. The bank found out that the house had been built on a snake bed, but they tried to resell the house. The bank did finally pull it off the market once Animal Plant had aired a story about the house on their network. It was found out that the house was built over a snake den. That is why there were snakes in the walls.

I am going to college at ITT-tech. Institute. I put to use the skills that I have been learning in my classes to use in designing the house that I would have loved to build on the property that I was buying. I did it as part of a class project. The class was designed to teach me about architecture and what goes into designing the house. The building codes I had to follow when designing the house. The building codes are there to protect the persons living in the house and the building inspector has to sign off on the building permit saying that you followed those building codes and that the building is safe.

The class instructor, Kay Jones, gave out the design parameters for the house we needed to design as our final class project that semester. This was designed as a real life scenario that we would meet as a client and designer. Listening to the client and incorporating the client's wishes is an important part of the design process. The parameters of the project were what I used in designing my house for my Architecture 1 class that I needed to take for my Computer Drafting& Design degree.

The project was a 1500 to 2000 sq. ft. one story house. A married couple with one child and expandable if needed in the future. A Family room and kitchen big enough to accommodate parties and social get together. The house I decided on was a three bedroom, two and a half bathroom and was almost 2000 sq. ft. one story house. A large two car garage that measured 20 ft. x 25 ft. The project also allowed me to be both the client and the designer, which allowed me to design a house that I would love to build for myself.

Money problems didn't allow me to keep the land I had to turn it back to Sunset Ranch, but I will try again one day. It was a land financing deal

I had with Sunset Ranch. I still have the plans for the house I would like to build.

Civil drafting is one of my classes in Computer Drafting and Design that I am taking to get my Associate of Science. The house I designed for the land in El Paso. I took it and added to the site plan that I designed. I can see how the house would have looked on the land that I was purchasing in El Paso, TX.

The house and site can be designed to meet the LEED qualifications. It would be a great location for green energy because it has no energy source being the property is out in the country. Setting up power to the land and house can be very expensive. I have gotten back in the market in El Paso, TX knowing more about my goals with a better network and partners behind me now. I will once again set it up to see how it looks and add to the land I am buying.

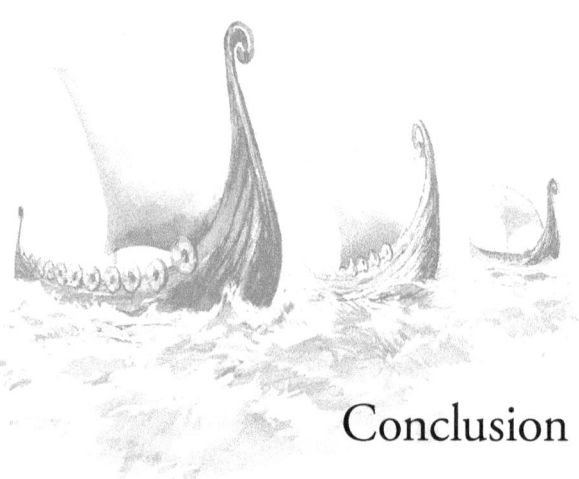

# Conclusion

I am hard on myself and some days I am even unhappy with myself and the position I find myself in a lot of days. I do drive myself and I do want to be happy but I am unhappy with myself when I don't succeed at what I want for myself. I demand more from myself then I do other people that I have worked with, and that is how I am when it comes to work, business and my personal life. I do believe that I deserve to be wealthy, and that I do deserve to be successful. A good foundation is where everything starts from.

It is nice to have that mentor/coach that will push you to achieve the needed steps to obtain that success you are looking for. They will also hold your feet to the fire when you fail or slack off and don't reach the goal that has been set for you. Sometimes self-discipline just isn't enough and you need that added extra push to get you there where you want to be. That also can spell the difference between success and failure. Success is different for everyone, and everyone defines success differently in their own lives.

One book or person can't define success for that person each and every one has to find that success for themselves. For me success wasn't living paycheck to paycheck. Success for me would be living a comfortable and enjoyable life with no worries. It want more than my parents and as kids we all want more and to be able to live better than are parents did. That would mean I am living a successful life.

I do have my days where the old defeating mindset comes through me and I have to try and overcome that old mindset. The Navy had their way in reinforcing and building that winning mindset it was also a way they built team work and character. Character and mindset as well wanting it bad enough pushed me to get my Associates of Arts in Business Admin.

My Norwegian Ancestors were a strong and hardy people with a strong mind and character that helped them achieve great things.

Getting caught by my grand-ma was a defining character building moment that I do tell people about. Since then and the more I have thought about it over the years the more I have felt that I deserved the spanking I got that day. My grand-ma was from the old school where even the grandparents disciplined the kids if they needed it.

I really wasn't showing much character Friday afternoon when put on the spot by Terry and Tom in front of another co-worker who had just started working there that day. I was put on the spot and not really sure what to say or how to answer the questions they were asking. I should have never said anything about Jason but when I did. There should have never been the open end answer that could have been interpreted any way they felt like interpreting it. Always make your answers to a question so that there is no room for misunderstanding or misinterpretation. Be a good partner and co-worker and don't try cause friction between other co-workers by twisting what the other person had intended to say.

My mom tried to hold my feet to the fire when I was taking on different lawns to mow but the excess were coming easier and easier. Especially if it was hot out or it had rained that day I knew they counted on me to mow their lawn, but the excesses came why I couldn't do it. I didn't know what a brand was and I had no one to teach me what a brand was or even fully understood what a brand was. My parents didn't with their limited education and all they taught was how to work for a paycheck. I had an economics explain it this that you are prostituting yourself for a paycheck. That made good sense to me in a lot of ways, because we are at the mercy of the employer to pay us what they want to pay us.

My cattle business was going better, but the main things that made it a failure were that I had no one to help me. I was in the military, and I was trying to take care of a business long distance. I had no to help me work the business and I was told one the calves got out and one had died. The ex-wife was no help to me because all she wanted to do is spend the money and let other people do the work. People working against you are a recipe for failure every time. I had to sell out so I didn't have the worry of the cattle business. Trust was another factor in my decision to sell out. Trust has to be there for it to be a successful business relationship.

I am building a stronger brand one block at a time and a lot smarter than before because I have learned more over the years. I am applying a lot of the things I have learned from other failure to building a successful brand from the ground up. The brand will be bigger and better than even once it is complete and fully in operation. I have embraced the information age and I have been making my presence seen on the internet. The information age has made a lot of older companies innovate, adapt and embrace the new technology. There is also one other thing that you need to be.

Be a polished communicator, because with lots of practice and rehearsals make for a polished communicator. All of the great polished communicators such as Ben Franklin, George Washington, Steve Jobs and Donald J. Trump, take the time to rehearse and practice before they make any speech or presentation or pitch to investors or a large crowd that is there to hear them speak.

There has been a lot companies close their doors because they couldn't innovate, adapt and embrace the new technology age fast enough. The information has to be shifted through because there is so much information out there and it is not all accurate information. The old model of the print newspapers and magazines are the main old brands having the roughest time adapting to the information age. That is why the information age can make or break a company very quickly. That is why a company must learn to innovate very quickly or be left behind very quickly by someone who has been innovating quickly.

A strong network can hold your feet to the fire and it also can help you find and get the best deals out there. You have to be able to act on those deals and that means having a good foundation to work from. Two key ingredients is good credit and the financial resources without them you will not be able to act up on the good deals. Those deals will just pass you by then, and someone in the right position will be able to act upon them. Take pride in the littlest of things because you never know who is looking at your work. The littlest of things can mean the difference between a successful brand and a brand that's a failure.

A good leader is one who listens, analyze and takes in the best advice of those people the owner or person in charge has surround himself with. One should not rigid, egotistical, and close mind that he doesn't listen to those people around him, and if he isn't go to listen to them in the first place then why surround yourself with good talent. I used to think it was bad to have to change your mind in mid-task but I look at as a change in a new direction that can make the out of the task a lot better in the end. Better means that the task gets done right the first time around and also means you don't have to spend more money doing it all over again.

The winning mind set is about being in alignment with your inner most truth and once you are in alignment with your inner most truth. You will not feel out of alignment with yourself and feel like you are fighting against yourself. It is all about being who you truly are inside and on the outside. Imagine you are living a life where you are not in conflict with your own self, so live a life where you are in true alignment and not in conflict with yourself.

Leave you with two pieces of Norse wisdom.

*Take care of your speech; it can be the catalyst for many needless problems. You never know who could be lending an ear to your ramblings.*

*What will be etched into history about your life? What legend will be left long after your gone? How have you made the world better?*

Ponder these questions daily.

# John H. Olsen
# Recommended Reading

*The Art of War written by Sun Tzu*

Compiled in the 6<sup>th</sup> century B.C. it is the oldest surviving military treatise.

*Think and Grow Rich written by Napoleon Hill*

Moneymaking secret that has made fortunes for more than five hundred exceedingly wealthy people whom I have carefully analyzed over a long period of years.

*Increase Your Financial IQ: Get smarter with your money written by Robert T. Kiyosaki*

It explains why financial is important today more than ever. In this world of financial turbulence, your best asset is your financial IQ.

*Why we want you to be rich written by Donald J. Trump and Robert T. Kiyosaki*

Two men have one message about financial education can only solve your money problems, and why they want you to be rich.

*The Trump Card written by Ivanka Trump*

Playing to win in work and life.

*Secrets of Closing the Sale written by Zig Ziglar*

Break down the price and question to persuade the people to close the deal or sale.

*The Art of the Deal written by Donald J. Trump*

Written in 1987, it is a story about his life and the biggest deals of his life.

*The Trumps written by Gwenda Blair*

Written in 2000, it is about the three generations of Trumps who built the Trump Empire.

*Lone Survivor: The eyewitness account of Operation Redwing and the lost heros of Seal Team 10 written by Marcus Luttrell*

Written in 2007, it about Operation Redwing and the heroes who were lost fighting the Taliban and Al Qaeda in Afghanistan

# Sources

Webster's New World Pocket Dictionary (4th Edition), copyright 2000, Wiley publishing, Inc. Cleveland, OH

24 Norse life rules, Red Frost motivation

.

www.ingramcontent.com/pod-product-compliance
Lightning Source LLC
Chambersburg PA
CBHW051238120626
46547CB00014B/1699